The Literary Life KIDS Commonplace Book

The Literary Life Podcast

Angelina Stanford
Cindy Rollins
Thomas Banks

The Literary Life KIDS Commonplace Book: Fairy Tale

By Angelina Stanford, Cindy Rollins, and Thomas Banks

Cover Art: Arthur Rackham, Illustration from A Midsummer Night's Dream, 1908.

Published by Blue Sky Daisies
blueskydaisies.net

ISBN 13: 978-1-944435-15-8

The Literary Life KIDS Commonplace Book

This book belongs to:

____.

If found, please contact me at this number:

____.

The Literary Life Podcast Official **KIDS** Commonplace Book.
Stories will save the world.

Visit us online at www.theliterary.life.

Subscribe to our podcast.

Join the conversation on our Facebook community:
The Literary Life Podcast Discussion Group

Download the printable and shareable Literary Life Kids' Reading Challenge at www.theliterary.life.

Creating a Commonplace Habit

It looks like someone has handed you this journal to record the books you have read, your thoughts on those books, and even some quotes you especially enjoy from them. Sometimes journaling doesn't seem all that fun at first. It can even feel a bit like a chore, but I can assure you that looking back over past reading journals, books lists, and commonplace quotes is one of the fun things in life. You will not regret the time you spent thinking about the books you have read and recording a little bit about them.

In this journal you can do several things. You can keep a list of books you have read over time. It can be a one-year record or a much longer record. All you need to write is the title and the author and maybe a rating if you enjoy rating things.

You can also use this book to record written narrations[1] you did of certain books you especially enjoyed. A narration is different from a book review in that you aren't giving your opinion about the book; rather, you are recording what you remember from the book. A narration could be on a paragraph or a chapter but not the whole book. A narration can also be a drawing. I am a big fan of drawing since it causes us to develop the habit of attention.

Guess what? You only learn the things you pay attention to. Knowing you are going to draw or narrate can help you pay attention, and that is how you get smart. You don't have to be smart to get smart. Intelligence starts right where you are. It starts at the place you say, "I don't know." "I don't know" is the best place in the world, as that is where you get to learn new things. Every-

1 *See p. 140 for more information about narrations.*

body is standing at that place everyday. Smart people just embrace it rather than pretending they already know.

You can also do book reviews in this journal. A review would be how you felt about the whole book after you finished it. It is my hope that all your reviews are good reviews because you are reading 'all the right books,' but perhaps that is a little unrealistic. Sometimes writing a review of a bad book at least makes you feel better about the time spent in that awful book.

Stories will save the world.

Finally, you can also use this book to record passages you especially love. You might think you don't need to record them because you will remember, but unfortunately that is not usually the case. A commonplace book is quite simply a place to record the quotes you run across in your reading or even ideas or sentences you see somewhere else that you love. In a way a commonplace journal helps define who you are by the things you love. Learning to love the very best things is another way we grow and learn, at least that is what C.S. Lewis says, and I have found he is often right.

In the end I hope you get a chance to read across all kinds of genres (a genre is just the type of book you are reading like sci-fi, fiction, fantasy, poetry, etc.) this year and throughout your life. You might be surprised to like books you never expected to like. It is fun to have some easy books to read to keep your mind oiled, but it is also important to stretch yourself and read a few hard books, too. A reading journal can keep you accountable to yourself. Reading has been my chief joy in life and greatest hobby; I hope you can find joy in it as well! You won't regret it.

—Cindy Rollins,
for all of the Literary Life Podcast hosts.

Index

Record the main content of each page here for a handy reference.

Index

Index

Record the main content of each page here for a handy reference.

39.

40.

41.

42.

43.

44.

45.

46.

47.

48.

49.

50.

51.

52.

53.

54.

55.

56.

57.

Index

58.

59.

60.

61.

62.

63.

64.

65.

66.

67.

68.

69.

70.

71.

72.

73.

74.

75.

76.

Index

Record the main content of each page here for a handy reference.

Index

Index

Record the main content of each page here for a handy reference.

115.

116.

117.

118.

119.

120.

121.

122.

123.

124.

125.

126.

127.

128.

129.

130.

131.

132.

133.

Index

Reading Challenge • 19 Books in 2021

192021 Kids Challenge:	Title Chosen	Completed
A Book of Myths *Such as* Tanglewood Tales *by Nathaniel Hawthorne*	Enid Blyton Tales of Anchint Greece	
Five Fairy Tales *Any selection you like*	Grims faciy tales	
Five Poems by One Poet *Such as Robert Frost, Emily Dickinson, or any other poet*		
Read Aloud a Book to a Sibling or Friend		
A History Biography *Such as Signature Biographies or Landmark or Childhood of Famous Americans or others*		
A Book Recommended by a Grandparent or Older Person		
Ten Fables *Aesop is one author*		
A Book by an Author You've Never Read Before	N.D WiLson 100 cabords	
A 19th Century Classic Children's Book *Such as* The Jungle Book *or* Little Women *or many others*		
A Middle Ages Book *Written in or set in the Middle Ages or Renaissance.* Men of Iron *by Howard Pyle, for example.*		

Download a printable list at www.theliterary.life.

Reading Challenge • 19 Books in 2021/22

192021 Kids Challenge:	Title Chosen	Completed
A 20th Century Classic Children's Book *The Chronicles of Narnia were written in the 20th century along with many others*		
A Book You Have Avoided		
Reread a Book		
A Biography of a Composer/Artist/Writer *You may like Opal Wheeler's artist biographies.*		
Five Tall Tales American Tall Tales *by Adrien Stoutenburg, for example*		
A Book Written in or Set in Ancient Greece or Rome		
A Mystery or a Detective Novel *Anything from Encyclopedia Brown to Dorothy L. Sayers!*	Harriet the Spy by Louise Fitzhugh	
A Legend *Such as King Arthur or Robin Hood. Rosemary Sutcliffe writes many books in this genre.*		
A Shakespeare Play *or a retelling of a Shakespeare play*		

Books I Want to Read

Fiction

Title Author Recommended by

Non-Fiction

Title Author Recommended by

Books I Want to Read / Listen to

Picture Books

Title	Author	Recommended by

Poetry

Title	Author	Recommended by

Books I Want to Read

Fairy Tales

Title	Author	Recommended by

Classic Works

Title	Author	Recommended by

Books I Want to Read

Devotional

Title	Author	Recommended by

Bestsellers

Title	Author	Recommended by

Reading Log

Title	Author	Date Read	Rating
			☆☆☆☆☆
			☆☆☆☆☆
			☆☆☆☆☆
			☆☆☆☆☆
			☆☆☆☆☆
			☆☆☆☆☆
			☆☆☆☆☆
			☆☆☆☆☆
			☆☆☆☆☆
			☆☆☆☆☆
			☆☆☆☆☆
			☆☆☆☆☆
			☆☆☆☆☆
			☆☆☆☆☆
			☆☆☆☆☆
			☆☆☆☆☆
			☆☆☆☆☆
			☆☆☆☆☆
			☆☆☆☆☆
			☆☆☆☆☆

Reading Log

Title	Author	Date Read	Rating
			☆☆☆☆☆
			☆☆☆☆☆
			☆☆☆☆☆
			☆☆☆☆☆
			☆☆☆☆☆
			☆☆☆☆☆
			☆☆☆☆☆
			☆☆☆☆☆
			☆☆☆☆☆
			☆☆☆☆☆
			☆☆☆☆☆
			☆☆☆☆☆
			☆☆☆☆☆
			☆☆☆☆☆
			☆☆☆☆☆
			☆☆☆☆☆
			☆☆☆☆☆
			☆☆☆☆☆
			☆☆☆☆☆
			☆☆☆☆☆

Reading Log

Title	Author	Date Read	Rating
			☆☆☆☆☆
			☆☆☆☆☆
			☆☆☆☆☆
			☆☆☆☆☆
			☆☆☆☆☆
			☆☆☆☆☆
			☆☆☆☆☆
			☆☆☆☆☆
			☆☆☆☆☆
			☆☆☆☆☆
			☆☆☆☆☆
			☆☆☆☆☆
			☆☆☆☆☆
			☆☆☆☆☆
			☆☆☆☆☆
			☆☆☆☆☆
			☆☆☆☆☆
			☆☆☆☆☆
			☆☆☆☆☆
			☆☆☆☆☆

Commonplace Quotes & Sketches

Commonplace Quotes & Sketches

Becus

"It is only with one's heart that one can see rightly. What is essential is invisible to the eye."
—*The Little Prince* by Antoine de Saint-Exupery

"'Why did you do all this for me?' he asked. 'I don't deserve it. I've never done anything for you.'
'You have been my friend,' replied Charlotte. 'That in itself is a tremendous thing.'"
—*Charlotte's Web* by E.B. White

Commonplace Quotes & Sketches

"'What makes the desert so beautiful,' said the little prince, 'is that somewhere it hides a well...'"
—*The Little Prince* by Antoine de Saint-Exupery

Commonplace Quotes & Sketches

"Finally the Rainbow Fish had only one shining scale left. His most prized possessions had been given away, yet he was very happy."
—*The Rainbow Fish* by Marcus Pfister

Commonplace Quotes & Sketches

"I love you right up to the moon—and back."
—*Guess How Much I Love You* by Sam McBratney

"Why, sometimes I've believed as many as six impossible things before breakfast."
—*Alice in Wonderland* by Lewis Carroll

Commonplace Quotes & Sketches

"Roads go ever on and on,
Over rock and under tree,
By caves where sun has never shone,
By streams that never find the sea;
Over snow by winter sown,
And through the merry flowers of June,
Over grass and over stone,
And under mountains in the moon."
—"Roads Go Ever On and On" by J.R.R. Tolkien

"'I'm afraid I can't put it more clearly,' Alice replied very politely, 'for I can't understand it myself to begin with; and being so many different sizes in a day is very confusing.'"

—*Alice's Adventures in Wonderland* by Lewis Carroll

Commonplace Quotes & Sketches

"'Real isn't how you are made,' said the Skin Horse. 'It's a thing that happens to you. When a child loves you for a long, long time, not just to play with, but REALLY loves you, then you become Real.'"
—*The Velveteen Rabbit* by Margery Williams

"'Does anybody here know how to spell "terrific"?'
'I think,' said the gander, 'it's tee double ee double rr double rr double eye double ff double eye double see see see see see.'"
—*Charlotte's Web* by E.B. White

"Animal crackers, and cocoa to drink,
That is the finest of suppers, I think;
When I'm grown up and can have what I please
I think I shall always insist upon these."
—"Animal Crackers" by Christopher Morley

Commonplace Quotes & Sketches

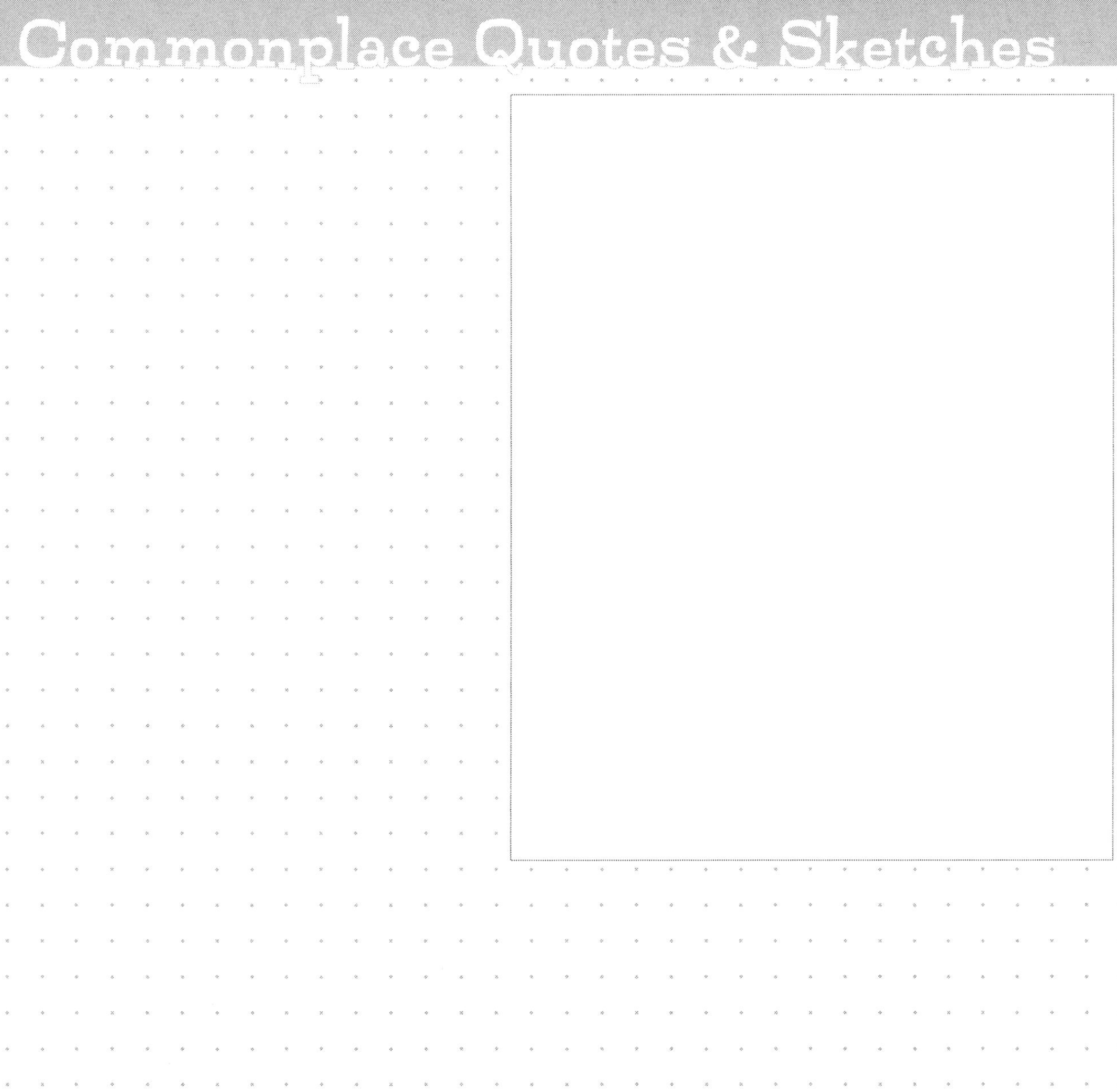

"'You should learn not to make personal remarks,' Alice said with some severity; 'it's very rude.'"
—*Alice's Adventures in Wonderland* by Lewis Carroll

Commonplace Quotes & Sketches

"Up the airy mountain,
down the rushy glen,
We daren't go a-hunting
for fear of little men;
Wee folk, good folk,
Trooping all together;
Green jacket, red cap,
And white owl's feather!"
—"The Fairies" by William Allingham

"But no one except Lucy knew that as it circled the mast it had whispered to her, 'Courage, dear heart.'"
—*The Voyage of the "Dawn Treader"* by C.S. Lewis

Commonplace Quotes & Sketches

"The Queen had only one way of settling all difficulties, great or small. 'Off with his head!' she said, without even looking round.
'I'll fetch the executioner myself,' said the King eagerly, and he hurried off."
—*Alice's Adventures in Wonderland* by Lewis Carroll

Commonplace Quotes & Sketches

"I shall find out thousands and thousands of things!"
—*The Secret Garden* by Frances Hodgson Burnett

"'Why did you call him Tortoise, if he wasn't one?' Alice asked.
'We called him Tortoise because he taught us,' said the Mock Turtle angrily: 'really you are very dull!'"
—*Alice's Adventures in Wonderland* by Lewis Carroll

Commonplace Quotes & Sketches

"You must never feel badly about making mistakes...as long as you take the trouble to learn from them. For you often learn more by being wrong for the right reasons than you do by being right for the wrong reasons."
—*The Phantom Tollbooth* by Norton Juster

Commonplace Quotes & Sketches

"Once there was an elephant,
Who tried to use the telephant—
No! no! I mean an elephone
Who tried to use the telephone—
(Dear me! I am not certain quite
That even now I've got it right.)"
—"Eletelephony" by Laura E. Richards

Commonplace Quotes & Sketches

"And the next day, as soon as it began to grow dusk, he went to the tower and cried, 'Oh Rapunzel, Rapunzel! Let down your hair.' And she let down her hair, and the King's son climbed up by it."

—"Rapunzel" in Grimm's Complete Fairy Tales

Commonplace Quotes & Sketches

"Day after day, day after day,
We stuck, nor breath nor motion;
As idle as a painted ship
Upon a painted ocean.

"Water, water, every where,
And all the boards did shrink;
Water, water, every where,
Nor any drop to drink."

—"The Rime of the Ancient Mariner" by Samuel Taylor Coleridge

Commonplace Quotes & Sketches

"'This is it, Merlin,' Arthur whispered. 'This will be my hub. We'll gather round this table as equals. Like spokes of a great wheel, the light of Truth shall radiate out through our brotherhood, to touch all who long for justice, honor, and mercy.'"
—*King Arthur and the Round Table* by Hudson Talbott

"Then [the huntsman] went into the room, and walked up to the bed, and saw the wolf lying there. 'At last I find you, you old sinner!' said he; 'I have been looking for you a long time.'"

—"Little Red Riding Hood" in Grimm's Complete Fairy Tales

Commonplace Quotes & Sketches

"When he reached the hayfield, everyone stopped work. They stood in the shade of an oak and pushed back their hats; and passed the dipper from hand to hand till all the egg-nog was gone. Almanzo drank his full share. The breeze seemed cool now, and Lazy John said, wiping the foam from his mustache, 'Ah! That puts heart into a man!'"
—*Farmer Boy* by Laura Ingalls Wilder

"Of course Hansel had not been looking at his kitten, but had been taking every now and then a flint from his pocket and dropping it on the road."
—"Hansel and Gretel" in Grimm's Complete Fairy Tales

"With Merlin's magical assistance, a spectacular palace swiftly rose upon enchanted meadows where the ancient fairy folk once abided. In their honor Arthur named his home as the Old Ones had called their domain, Camelot."
—*King Arthur and the Round Table* by Hudson Talbott

Commonplace Quotes & Sketches

"The Rat danced up and down in the road, simply transported with passion. 'You villains!' he shouted, shaking both fists, 'You scoundrels, you highwaymen, you—you—road-hogs!—I'll have the law on you! I'll report you! I'll take you through all the Courts!'"
—*The Wind in the Willows* by Kenneth Grahame

"When it was morning, and Snow-White awoke and saw the seven dwarfs, she was very frightened; but they seemed quite friendly, and asked her what her name was, and she told them; and then they asked how she came to be in their house."
—"Snow-White and the Seven Dwarfs" in Grimm's Complete Fairy Tales

"Meanwhile, word spread throughout the world that the new High King of all Britain was assemblng an extraordinary court. From near and far, knights and nobles rode forth to Camelot, hoping to prove themselves worthy of this splendid new company."
—*King Arthur and the Round Table* by Hudson Talbott

"Sam said, 'Bah! Only a weakling gives up when he's becalmed! A strong man sails by ash breeze!'"
—*Carry On, Mr. Bowditch* by Jean Lee Latham

"...Cinderella went again to her mother's grave, and said to the tree,

'Little tree, little tree, shake over me,
That silver and gold may come down and cover me.'

Then the bird cast down a dress, the like of which had never been seen for splendor and brilliancy, and slippers that were of gold...And when she appeared in this dress at the feast nobody knew what to say for wonderment."

—"Cinderella" in Grimm's Complete Fairy Tales

"The trouble with a kitten is
THAT
Eventually it becomes a
CAT."
—"The Kitten" by Ogden Nash

Commonplace Quotes & Sketches

"They stood on the snowy pond, in their tall boots and plaid jackets and fur caps with fur ear-muffs, and the frost of their breaths was on their long mustaches. Each had an ax on his shoulder, and they carried cross-cut saws."

—*Farmer Boy* by Laura Ingalls Wilder

Commonplace Quotes & Sketches

"Said the Mock Turtle: 'why, if a fish came to *me*, and told me he was going a journey, I should say, 'With what porpoise?'
'Don't you mean "purpose"?' said Alice.
'I mean what I say,' the Mock Turtle replied in an offended tone."
—*Alice's Adventures in Wonderland* by Lewis Carroll

"I don't understand it any more than you do, but one thing I've learned is that you don't have to understand things for them to be."
—*A Wrinkle in Time* by Madeleine L'Engle

"How doth the little crocodile
Improve his shining tail,
And pour the waters of the Nile
On every golden scale!"
—*Alice's Adventures in Wonderland* by Lewis Carroll

"'What day is it?' asked Winnie the Pooh.
'It's today,' squeaked Piglet.
'My favorite day,' said Pooh."
—*The Adventures of Winnie the Pooh* by A. A. Milne

"Who knows, my friend? Maybe the sword does have some magic. Personally, I think it's the warrior who wields it."
—*Redwall* by Brian Jacques

"'Once you were a tiny seed—a papoose wrapped in white down. Your cradleboard swung from a twig. Then a strong Summer Wind came by. He lifted you from your mother's arms and brought you here. You see,' laughed the boy, 'I understand tree-talk! And I think he was a wise Wind. He planted your seed in this mud among sharp-edged rocks, where buffalo do not like to walk. But soon now they will reach over the rocks to scratch themselves against your branches. I'll make a stockade to protect you!' And the boy piled rocks higher around the lone sapling."
—*The Tree in the Trail* by Holling C. Holling

Commonplace Quotes & Sketches

"One of the major advantages a cowdog has over a cat is that your ordinary run-of-the-mill cat is flighty and impulsive, while your cowdog applies mental discipline to every problem. I think most experts would back me up on this."
—*The Further Adventures of Hank the Cowdog* by John Erickson

"'It doesn't happen all at once,' he said. 'You become. It takes a long time. That's why it doesn't often happen to people who break easily, or have sharp edges, or who have to be carefully kept. Generally, by the time you are Real, most of your hair has been loved off, and your eyes drop out and you get loose in the joints and very shabby. But these things don't matter at all, because once you are Real you can't be ugly, except to people who don't understand.'"

—*The Velveteen Rabbit* by Margery Williams

"'Well, Sir, if things are real, they're there all the time.'
'Are they?' said the Professor; and Peter did not know quite what to say."
—*The Lion, the Witch, and the Wardrobe* by C.S. Lewis

Commonplace Quotes & Sketches

"Keep all your promises, don't take what doesn't belong to you, and always look after those less fortunate than yourself, and you'll do well in the world."

—*The Dragon of Lonely Island* by Rebecca Rupp

"'The Silver Shoes,' said the Good Witch, 'have wonderful powers...All you have to do is to knock the heels together three times and command the shoes to carry you wherever you wish to go.'"
—*The Wizard of Oz* by L. Frank Baum

"'Hallo, Rabbit,' he said, 'is that you?'
'Let's pretend it isn't,' said Rabbit, 'and see what happens.'"
—*The Adventures of Winnie the Pooh* by A. A. Milne

Commonplace Quotes & Sketches

"There is nothing sweeter in this sad world than the sound of someone you love calling your name."
—*The Tale of Despereaux* by Kate DiCamillo

"Peter did not feel very brave; indeed, he felt he was going to be sick. But that made no difference to what he had to do."
—*The Lion, the Witch, and the Wardrobe* by C.S. Lewis

"On Monday, when the sun is hot
I wonder to myself a lot:
'Now is it true, or is it not,
That what is which and which is what?'"
—*The Adventures of Winnie the Pooh* by A. A. Milne

Commonplace Quotes & Sketches

"Flintlocks are loaded from muzzle. A small spoonful of gunpowder is sifted in, followed by 'ball' (lead bullet), wrapped in a tiny square of greased cloth or buckskin-the 'patch,' rammed down with ramrod. 'Pan' is 'primed.' Hammer strikes a few sparks with 'flint' on 'steel'—fire from priming goes through a hole in barrel, and gun 'fires.'"
—*The Tree in the Trail* by Holling C. Holling

"'But if you will come to me tomorrow morning, I will stuff your head with brains. I cannot tell you how to use them, however, you must find that out for yourself,' [said Oz.]"
—*The Wizard of Oz* by L. Frank Baum

Commonplace Quotes & Sketches

"'Child,' said the Voice, 'I am telling you your story, not hers. I tell no one any story but his own.'"
—*The Horse and His Boy* by C.S. Lewis

"He was a huge man in a bright red robe (bright as holly-berries) with a hood that had fur inside it and a great white beard that fell like a foamy waterfall over his chest... Some of the pictures of Father Christmas in our world make him look only funny and jolly. But now that the children actually stood looking at him they didn't find it quite like that. He was so big and so glad, and so real, that they all became quite still. They felt very glad, but also solemn."
—*The Lion, the Witch, and the Wardrobe* by C.S. Lewis

"It had a door made of a piece of tin-roofing, and there was a smokestack going up through the ceiling. Inside was a sort of bench where you could lie down, and we had two old butter-crates for chairs. We put dry hay down on the floor for carpet, and under the hay there was a secret hole where we could hide anything that was specially valuable."

—*Owls in the Family* by Farley Mowat

Commonplace Quotes & Sketches

"Custard the dragon had big sharp teeth,
And spikes on top of him and scales underneath,
Mouth like a fireplace, chimney for a nose,
And realio, trulio daggers on his toes."
"The Tale of Custard the Dragon" by Ogden Nash

Commonplace Quotes & Sketches

"No act of kindness, no matter how small, is ever wasted."
—"The Lion and the Mouse" by Aesop

Narrations

Narration

Title:

Author:

Type of book:

Non-fiction: history, biography, how-to, science, other

Fiction: myth, legend, fairy tale, fable, novel, science fiction, fantasy, other

Poetry: narrative, lyric, ballad, sonnet, other

Reading challenge category (if applicable):

My Narration:

Narration

Title:

Author:

Type of book:

Non-fiction: history, biography, how-to, science, other

Fiction: myth, legend, fairy tale, fable, novel, science fiction, fantasy, other

Poetry: narrative, lyric, ballad, sonnet, other

Reading challenge category (if applicable):

My Narration:

Narration

Title:

Author:

Type of book:

Non-fiction: history, biography, how-to, science, other

Fiction: myth, legend, fairy tale, fable, novel, science fiction, fantasy, other

Poetry: narrative, lyric, ballad, sonnet, other

Reading challenge category (if applicable):

My Narration:

Narration

Title:

Author:

Type of book:

Non-fiction: history, biography, how-to, science, other

Fiction: myth, legend, fairy tale, fable, novel, science fiction, fantasy, other

Poetry: narrative, lyric, ballad, sonnet, other

Reading challenge category (if applicable):

My Narration:

Narration

Title:

Author:

Type of book:

Non-fiction: history, biography, how-to, science, other

Fiction: myth, legend, fairy tale, fable, novel, science fiction, fantasy, other

Poetry: narrative, lyric, ballad, sonnet, other

Reading challenge category (if applicable):

My Narration:

Narration

Title:

Author:

Type of book:

Non-fiction: history, biography, how-to, science, other

Fiction: myth, legend, fairy tale, fable, novel, science fiction, fantasy, other

Poetry: narrative, lyric, ballad, sonnet, other

Reading challenge category (if applicable):

My Narration:

Narration

Title:

Author:

Type of book:

Non-fiction: history, biography, how-to, science, other

Fiction: myth, legend, fairy tale, fable, novel, science fiction, fantasy, other

Poetry: narrative, lyric, ballad, sonnet, other

Reading challenge category (if applicable):

My Narration:

Narration

Title:

Author:

Type of book:

Non-fiction: history, biography, how-to, science, other

Fiction: myth, legend, fairy tale, fable, novel, science fiction, fantasy, other

Poetry: narrative, lyric, ballad, sonnet, other

Reading challenge category (if applicable):

My Narration:

Narration

Title:

Author:

Type of book:

Non-fiction: history, biography, how-to, science, other

Fiction: myth, legend, fairy tale, fable, novel, science fiction, fantasy, other

Poetry: narrative, lyric, ballad, sonnet, other

Reading challenge category (if applicable):

My Narration:

Narration

Title:

Author:

Type of book:

Non-fiction: history, biography, how-to, science, other

Fiction: myth, legend, fairy tale, fable, novel, science fiction, fantasy, other

Poetry: narrative, lyric, ballad, sonnet, other

Reading challenge category (if applicable):

My Narration:

Narration

Title:

Author:

Type of book:

Non-fiction: history, biography, how-to, science, other

Fiction: myth, legend, fairy tale, fable, novel, science fiction, fantasy, other

Poetry: narrative, lyric, ballad, sonnet, other

Reading challenge category (if applicable):

My Narration:

Narration

Title:

Author:

Type of book:

Non-fiction: history, biography, how-to, science, other

Fiction: myth, legend, fairy tale, fable, novel, science fiction, fantasy, other

Poetry: narrative, lyric, ballad, sonnet, other

Reading challenge category (if applicable):

My Narration:

Narration

Title:

Author:

Type of book:

Non-fiction: history, biography, how-to, science, other

Fiction: myth, legend, fairy tale, fable, novel, science fiction, fantasy, other

Poetry: narrative, lyric, ballad, sonnet, other

Reading challenge category (if applicable):

My Narration:

Narration

Title:

Author:

Type of book:

Non-fiction: history, biography, how-to, science, other

Fiction: myth, legend, fairy tale, fable, novel, science fiction, fantasy, other

Poetry: narrative, lyric, ballad, sonnet, other

Reading challenge category (if applicable):

My Narration:

Narration

Title:

Author:

Type of book:

Non-fiction: history, biography, how-to, science, other

Fiction: myth, legend, fairy tale, fable, novel, science fiction, fantasy, other

Poetry: narrative, lyric, ballad, sonnet, other

Reading challenge category (if applicable):

My Narration:

Narration

Title:

Author:

Type of book:

Non-fiction: history, biography, how-to, science, other

Fiction: myth, legend, fairy tale, fable, novel, science fiction, fantasy, other

Poetry: narrative, lyric, ballad, sonnet, other

Reading challenge category (if applicable):

My Narration:

Narration

Title:

Author:

Type of book:

Non-fiction: history, biography, how-to, science, other

Fiction: myth, legend, fairy tale, fable, novel, science fiction, fantasy, other

Poetry: narrative, lyric, ballad, sonnet, other

Reading challenge category (if applicable):

My Narration:

Narration

Title:

Author:

Type of book:

Non-fiction: history, biography, how-to, science, other

Fiction: myth, legend, fairy tale, fable, novel, science fiction, fantasy, other

Poetry: narrative, lyric, ballad, sonnet, other

Reading challenge category (if applicable):

My Narration:

Narration

Title:

Author:

Type of book:

Non-fiction: history, biography, how-to, science, other

Fiction: myth, legend, fairy tale, fable, novel, science fiction, fantasy, other

Poetry: narrative, lyric, ballad, sonnet, other

Reading challenge category (if applicable):

My Narration:

Narration

Title:

Author:

Type of book:

Non-fiction: history, biography, how-to, science, other

Fiction: myth, legend, fairy tale, fable, novel, science fiction, fantasy, other

Poetry: narrative, lyric, ballad, sonnet, other

Reading challenge category (if applicable):

My Narration:

Narration

Title:

Author:

Type of book:

Non-fiction: history, biography, how-to, science, other

Fiction: myth, legend, fairy tale, fable, novel, science fiction, fantasy, other

Poetry: narrative, lyric, ballad, sonnet, other

Reading challenge category (if applicable):

My Narration:

Narration

Title:

Author:

Type of book:

Non-fiction: history, biography, how-to, science, other

Fiction: myth, legend, fairy tale, fable, novel, science fiction, fantasy, other

Poetry: narrative, lyric, ballad, sonnet, other

Reading challenge category (if applicable):

My Narration:

Narration

Title:

Author:

Type of book:

Non-fiction: history, biography, how-to, science, other

Fiction: myth, legend, fairy tale, fable, novel, science fiction, fantasy, other

Poetry: narrative, lyric, ballad, sonnet, other

Reading challenge category (if applicable):

My Narration:

Narration

Title:

Author:

Type of book:

Non-fiction: history, biography, how-to, science, other

Fiction: myth, legend, fairy tale, fable, novel, science fiction, fantasy, other

Poetry: narrative, lyric, ballad, sonnet, other

Reading challenge category (if applicable):

My Narration:

Narration

Title:

Author:

Type of book:

Non-fiction: history, biography, how-to, science, other

Fiction: myth, legend, fairy tale, fable, novel, science fiction, fantasy, other

Poetry: narrative, lyric, ballad, sonnet, other

Reading challenge category (if applicable):

My Narration:

Narration

Title:

Author:

Type of book:

Non-fiction: history, biography, how-to, science, other

Fiction: myth, legend, fairy tale, fable, novel, science fiction, fantasy, other

Poetry: narrative, lyric, ballad, sonnet, other

Reading challenge category (if applicable):

My Narration:

Narration

Title:

Author:

Type of book:

Non-fiction: history, biography, how-to, science, other

Fiction: myth, legend, fairy tale, fable, novel, science fiction, fantasy, other

Poetry: narrative, lyric, ballad, sonnet, other

Reading challenge category (if applicable):

My Narration:

Narration

Title:

Author:

Type of book:

Non-fiction: history, biography, how-to, science, other

Fiction: myth, legend, fairy tale, fable, novel, science fiction, fantasy, other

Poetry: narrative, lyric, ballad, sonnet, other

Reading challenge category (if applicable):

My Narration:

Narration

Title:

Author:

Type of book:

Non-fiction: history, biography, how-to, science, other

Fiction: myth, legend, fairy tale, fable, novel, science fiction, fantasy, other

Poetry: narrative, lyric, ballad, sonnet, other

Reading challenge category (if applicable):

My Narration:

Book Reviews

My Review

Title:

Date Read:

Author:

Rating: ☆ ☆ ☆ ☆ ☆

Type of book:

Non-fiction: history, biography, how-to, science, other

Fiction: myth, legend, fairy tale, fable, novel, science fiction, fantasy, other

Poetry: narrative, lyric, ballad, sonnet, other

Reading challenge category (if applicable):

My Review

Title:

Author:

Date Read:

Rating: ☆ ☆ ☆ ☆ ☆

Type of book:

Non-fiction: history, biography, how-to, science, other

Fiction: myth, legend, fairy tale, fable, novel, science fiction, fantasy, other

Poetry: narrative, lyric, ballad, sonnet, other

Reading challenge category (if applicable):

My Review

Title:

Date Read:

Author:

Rating: ☆ ☆ ☆ ☆ ☆

Type of book:

Non-fiction: history, biography, how-to, science, other

Fiction: myth, legend, fairy tale, fable, novel, science fiction, fantasy, other

Poetry: narrative, lyric, ballad, sonnet, other

Reading challenge category (if applicable):

My Review

Title:

Author:

Date Read:

Rating: ☆ ☆ ☆ ☆ ☆

Type of book:

Non-fiction: history, biography, how-to, science, other

Fiction: myth, legend, fairy tale, fable, novel, science fiction, fantasy, other

Poetry: narrative, lyric, ballad, sonnet, other

Reading challenge category (if applicable):

My Review

Title:

Author:

Date Read:

Rating: ☆ ☆ ☆ ☆ ☆

Type of book:

Non-fiction: history, biography, how-to, science, other

Fiction: myth, legend, fairy tale, fable, novel, science fiction, fantasy, other

Poetry: narrative, lyric, ballad, sonnet, other

Reading challenge category (if applicable):

My Review

Title:

Author:

Date Read:

Rating: ☆ ☆ ☆ ☆ ☆

Type of book:

Non-fiction: history, biography, how-to, science, other

Fiction: myth, legend, fairy tale, fable, novel, science fiction, fantasy, other

Poetry: narrative, lyric, ballad, sonnet, other

Reading challenge category (if applicable):

My Review

Title:

Author:

Date Read:

Rating: ☆ ☆ ☆ ☆ ☆

Type of book:

Non-fiction: history, biography, how-to, science, other

Fiction: myth, legend, fairy tale, fable, novel, science fiction, fantasy, other

Poetry: narrative, lyric, ballad, sonnet, other

Reading challenge category (if applicable):

My Review

Title:

Author:

Date Read:

Rating: ☆ ☆ ☆ ☆ ☆

Type of book:

Non-fiction: history, biography, how-to, science, other

Fiction: myth, legend, fairy tale, fable, novel, science fiction, fantasy, other

Poetry: narrative, lyric, ballad, sonnet, other

Reading challenge category (if applicable):

My Review

Title:

Date Read:

Author:

Rating: ☆ ☆ ☆ ☆ ☆

Type of book:

Non-fiction: history, biography, how-to, science, other

Fiction: myth, legend, fairy tale, fable, novel, science fiction, fantasy, other

Poetry: narrative, lyric, ballad, sonnet, other

Reading challenge category (if applicable):

My Review

Title:

Author:

Date Read:

Rating: ☆ ☆ ☆ ☆ ☆

Type of book:

Non-fiction: history, biography, how-to, science, other

Fiction: myth, legend, fairy tale, fable, novel, science fiction, fantasy, other

Poetry: narrative, lyric, ballad, sonnet, other

Reading challenge category (if applicable):

My Review

Title:

Date Read:

Author:

Rating: ☆ ☆ ☆ ☆ ☆

Type of book:

Non-fiction: history, biography, how-to, science, other

Fiction: myth, legend, fairy tale, fable, novel, science fiction, fantasy, other

Poetry: narrative, lyric, ballad, sonnet, other

Reading challenge category (if applicable):

My Review

Title:

Author:

Date Read:

Rating: ☆ ☆ ☆ ☆ ☆

Type of book:

Non-fiction: history, biography, how-to, science, other

Fiction: myth, legend, fairy tale, fable, novel, science fiction, fantasy, other

Poetry: narrative, lyric, ballad, sonnet, other

Reading challenge category (if applicable):

My Review

Title:

Date Read:

Author:

Rating:

Type of book:

Non-fiction: history, biography, how-to, science, other

Fiction: myth, legend, fairy tale, fable, novel, science fiction, fantasy, other

Poetry: narrative, lyric, ballad, sonnet, other

Reading challenge category (if applicable):

My Review

Title:

Author:

Date Read:

Rating: ☆ ☆ ☆ ☆ ☆

Type of book:

Non-fiction: history, biography, how-to, science, other

Fiction: myth, legend, fairy tale, fable, novel, science fiction, fantasy, other

Poetry: narrative, lyric, ballad, sonnet, other

Reading challenge category (if applicable):

My Review

Title:

Date Read:

Author:

Rating: ☆ ☆ ☆ ☆ ☆

Type of book:

Non-fiction: history, biography, how-to, science, other

Fiction: myth, legend, fairy tale, fable, novel, science fiction, fantasy, other

Poetry: narrative, lyric, ballad, sonnet, other

Reading challenge category (if applicable):

My Review

Title:

Author:

Date Read:

Rating: ☆ ☆ ☆ ☆ ☆

Type of book:

Non-fiction: history, biography, how-to, science, other

Fiction: myth, legend, fairy tale, fable, novel, science fiction, fantasy, other

Poetry: narrative, lyric, ballad, sonnet, other

Reading challenge category (if applicable):

My Review

Title:

Date Read:

Author:

Rating: ☆ ☆ ☆ ☆ ☆

Type of book:

Non-fiction: history, biography, how-to, science, other

Fiction: myth, legend, fairy tale, fable, novel, science fiction, fantasy, other

Poetry: narrative, lyric, ballad, sonnet, other

Reading challenge category (if applicable):

My Review

Title:

Author:

Date Read:

Rating: ☆ ☆ ☆ ☆ ☆

Type of book:

Non-fiction: history, biography, how-to, science, other

Fiction: myth, legend, fairy tale, fable, novel, science fiction, fantasy, other

Poetry: narrative, lyric, ballad, sonnet, other

Reading challenge category (if applicable):

My Review

Title:

Date Read:

Author:

Rating: ☆ ☆ ☆ ☆ ☆

Type of book:

Non-fiction: history, biography, how-to, science, other

Fiction: myth, legend, fairy tale, fable, novel, science fiction, fantasy, other

Poetry: narrative, lyric, ballad, sonnet, other

Reading challenge category (if applicable):

My Review

Title:

Author:

Date Read:

Rating: ☆ ☆ ☆ ☆ ☆

Type of book:

Non-fiction: history, biography, how-to, science, other

Fiction: myth, legend, fairy tale, fable, novel, science fiction, fantasy, other

Poetry: narrative, lyric, ballad, sonnet, other

Reading challenge category (if applicable):

My Review

Title:

Author:

Date Read:

Rating: ☆ ☆ ☆ ☆ ☆

Type of book:

Non-fiction: history, biography, how-to, science, other

Fiction: myth, legend, fairy tale, fable, novel, science fiction, fantasy, other

Poetry: narrative, lyric, ballad, sonnet, other

Reading challenge category (if applicable):

My Review

Title:

Author:

Date Read:

Rating: ☆ ☆ ☆ ☆ ☆

Type of book:

Non-fiction: history, biography, how-to, science, other

Fiction: myth, legend, fairy tale, fable, novel, science fiction, fantasy, other

Poetry: narrative, lyric, ballad, sonnet, other

Reading challenge category (if applicable):

Title:

Author:

Date Read:

Rating: ☆ ☆ ☆ ☆ ☆

Type of book:

Non-fiction: history, biography, how-to, science, other

Fiction: myth, legend, fairy tale, fable, novel, science fiction, fantasy, other

Poetry: narrative, lyric, ballad, sonnet, other

Reading challenge category (if applicable):

My Review

Title:

Author:

Date Read:

Rating: ☆ ☆ ☆ ☆ ☆

Type of book:

Non-fiction: history, biography, how-to, science, other

Fiction: myth, legend, fairy tale, fable, novel, science fiction, fantasy, other

Poetry: narrative, lyric, ballad, sonnet, other

Reading challenge category (if applicable):

My Review

Title:

Date Read:

Author:

Rating: ☆ ☆ ☆ ☆ ☆

Type of book:

Non-fiction: history, biography, how-to, science, other

Fiction: myth, legend, fairy tale, fable, novel, science fiction, fantasy, other

Poetry: narrative, lyric, ballad, sonnet, other

Reading challenge category (if applicable):

Extras

Reading Challenge Ideas

What will you read for the challenge?

It's entirely up to you, of course! That's the fun! But sometimes it might be hard to think of something good for a particular category. So we'll throw out a few titles to get you started...

A Book of Myths
Such as *Tanglewood Tales* by Nathaniel Hawthorne. Also consider:

D'Aulaire's *Book of Greek Myths*
D'Aulaire's *Book of Norse Myths*
Mythology by Edith Hamilton
The Age of Fable by Bulfinch
The Children of Odin by Padriac Colum
The Heroes by Charles Kingsley

Five Fairy Tales
Any selection you like. Look for your fairy tales in collections like these:

Grimms' Fairy Tales
Blue Fairy Book
Hans Christian Andersen's Fairy Tales

Five Poems by One Poet
Such as Robert Frost, Emily Dickinson, or any other poet. Other poets and their poems to look for:

Walter de la Mare: especially "The Listeners," "Arabia," "Here Lies a Most Beautiful Lady," "Napoleon," and "Alexander"
Alfred, Lord Tennyson: especially "The Kraken," "Crossing the Bar," "Ask Me No More," "Now Sleeps the Crimson Petal," and "Ulysses"
William Wordsworth: especially the Lucy Poems, "Westminster Bridge," "Surprised by Joy"
William Butler Yeats: especially "The Song of Wandering Aengus," "An Irish Airman Foresees His Death," "The Lake Isle of Innisfree," "Politics," and "When You Are Old"

Read a Book Aloud to a Sibling or Friend

Madeline by Ludwig Bemelmans
The Little Prince by Antoine de Saint-Exupery

Charlotte's Web by E.B. White
Sarah, Plain and Tall by Patricia MacLachlan

A History Biography

Such as Signature Biographies, Landmark Biographies, or "Childhood of Famous Americans" or others.

People you might like to read about:

Abraham Lincoln or Francis Marion, etc
Clara Barton or Florence Nightingale
Thomas Edison or another inventor

Particular biographies you might enjoy:

A picture book biography—such as Diane Stanley's *Bard of Avon* (Shakespeare) or Cheryl Harness's *The Literary Adventures of Washington Irving: American Storyteller* and others
Helen Keller's autobiography *The Story of My Life*

A Book Recommended by a Grandparent or Older Person

Go ask for suggestions!

Ten Fables

Aesop is one author. Here are some particular editions of collections to consider:

Aesop's Fables by Jerry Pinkney
The Complete Fables by Aesop (Penguin Classics edition)
The Tortoise and the Geese and Other Fables of Bidpai by Maude Barrows Dutton

A Book by an Author You've Never Read Before

Maybe you have never read something by:

George MacDonald, such as *The Princess and the Goblin*
Gloria Whelan, such as *Angel on the Square*
Frances Hodgson Burnett, such as *The Secret Garden*

A 19th Century Children's Classic

Such as *The Jungle Book* or *Little Women* or many others

The Adventures of Tom Sawyer by Mark Twain
The Little Princess by Frances Hodgson Burnett
Alice in Wonderland by Lewis Carroll
Black Beauty by Anna Sewell
Story of the Treasure Seekers by Edith Nesbit

Reading Challenge Ideas

A Middle Ages Book

Written in or set in the Middle Ages or Renaissance.

Otto of the Silver Hand or *Men of Iron* by Howard Pyle
Stories of Beowulf by H.E. Marshall
I, Juan de Pareia by Elizabeth Borton DeTrevino
The White Company Sir Arthur Conan Doyle
The Black Arrow by Robert Louis Stevenson

A 20th Century Children's Classic

Any of the The Chronicles of Narnia books
Rebecca of Sunnybrook Farm by Kate Douglas Wiggin
Five Children and It by Edith Nesbit
The Trumpet of the Swan by E.B. White

A Book You Have Avoided

What are *you* avoiding?

Reread a Book

Grab a favorite!

A Biography of a Composer, Artist, or Writer

You may like Opal Wheeler's artist biographies, which include biographies of Bach, Beethoven, Chopin, Handel, Schubert, Mozart, and Tchaikovsky.
Consider biographies of Leonardo DaVinci, Michaelangelo, and Charles Dickens by Diane Stanley
A Boy Called Dickens by Deborah Hopkinson

Five Tall Tales

American Tall Tales by Adrien Stoutenburg, for example
Steven Kellogg picture books: *Paul Bunyan*, *Johnny Appleseed*, *Sally Ann Thunder Ann Whirlwind Crockett*
John Henry by Jerry Pinkney

A Book Written or Set in Ancient Greece or Rome

Black Ships Before Troy by Rosemary Sutcliff
Wanderings of Odysseus by Rosemary Sutcliff
Eagle of the Ninth by Rosemary Sutcliff

The Children's Homer by Padriac Colum
Jason and the Golden Fleece by Padriac Colum

A Mystery or Detective Novel
Anything from Encyclopedia Brown to Dorothy L. Sayers! Here are some ideas:
Enola Holmes series by Nancy Springer
The Boxcar Children by Gertrude Chandler Warner
Detectives in Togas by Henry Winterfeld
Mandie series by Lois Gladys Leppard

A Legend
Such as King Arthur or Robin Hood.
Rosemary Sutcliffe writes many books in this genre.
Myths and Legends by Rosemary Sutcliffe
Legends of King Arthur by Rosemary Sutcliffe
Look for books by authors Roger Lancelyn Green or Howard Pyle.

A Shakespeare Play
Or a retelling of a Shakespeare play
Look for versions by Edith Nesbit or Charles & Mary Lamb.
Picture books by Marcia Williams or Bruce Coville.

More Info

Narration might sound unfamiliar to you, but you probably practice narration every day without thinking much about it. If you come home from basketball practice and tell your family about the practice session, you are narrating. When you tell your friend about your family's vacation, you are narrating.

Narrating is a way of *telling* back to someone else about a story or real-life event that they didn't experience first-hand. When you write down what you "tell" about a story, it's called written narration. You can also draw pictures to tell about the story and make a picture narration.

About the Authors

Angelina Stanford

Angelina Stanford has an Honors Baccalaureate Degree and a Master's Degree in English Literature from the University of Louisiana, graduating Phi Kappa Phi. For over twenty-five years, she has shared her passion and enthusiasm for literature with students in a variety of settings and is a popular conference speaker and podcast guest. In 2020, with her husband, Thomas Banks, she founded the House of Humane Letters, providing classes, webinars, conferences and other resources for a more humane education. Angelina maintains a high commitment to teaching teachers and students the skill and art of reading well—and in recapturing the tradition of literary scholarship needed to fully engage with the Great Books. She is a great believer that Stories Will Save the World!

Cindy Rollins

Cindy Rollins homeschooled her nine children for over thirty years. She is a co-host with Angelina Stanford and Thomas Banks of the popular Literary Life Podcast and curates the "Over the Back Fence Newsletter" at CindyRollins.net. She is the author of *Mere Motherhood: Morning Time*, *Nursery Rhymes*, and *My Journey Toward Sanctification; A Handbook for Morning Time*; the *Mere Motherhood Newsletters*; and *Hallelujah: Cultivating Advent Traditions with Handel's Messiah*.

Cindy runs an active Patreon group where the participants read Charlotte Mason's volumes and discuss questions pertaining to motherhood and life. Her heart's desire is to encourage moms using Charlotte Mason's timeless principles. She lives in Chattanooga, Tennessee, with her husband, Tim, and dog, Max. She also travels around the country visiting her 13 grandchildren, watching her youngest son play baseball, and occasionally speaking at events.

Thomas Banks

Thomas Banks has taught great books with an emphasis on Greek and Roman literature, Latin grammar and ancient history for more than ten years both as a private tutor and as a junior high and high school teacher in his native Idaho and Montana. He holds a dual bachelor's degree in English Literature and Classical Studies from the University of Idaho, from which he graduated in 2008. In the summer of 2019, he moved to North Carolina to marry the illustrious Ms. Angelina Stanford, who said yes for some reason.

Poetry is a particular love of his, and he has published original verse and translations in First Things, the St. Austin Review and various other periodicals. His personal list of favorite writers never really stops growing, but will always include Homer, Euripides, Virgil, Ovid, St. Augustine, Shakespeare, Samuel Johnson, Byron, Keats, Walter Scott and Thomas Hardy. Of these and so many others one cannot have enough.

Thomas Banks currently resides in North Carolina, where he teaches Latin, literature and history online with his wife Angelina Stanford at The House of Humane Letters. His poetry, translations and other writings have appeared in First Things, The Imaginative Conservative, The New English Review, and various other publications.

Other Blue Sky Daisies Titles

Geography Books

Elementary Geography by Charlotte Mason

Home Geography for Primary Grades with Written and Oral Exercises by C. C. Long

Language Arts and Grammar Books

The Mother Tongue: Adapted for Modern Students by George Lyman Kittredge. In this series: Workbook 1 and 2; Answer Key 1 and 2

Exercises in Dictation by F. Peel

Grammar Land: Grammar in Fun for the Children of Schoolroom Shire (Annotated) By M. L. Nesbitt. Annotated by Amy M. Edwards and Christina J. Mugglin

The CopyWorkBook Series

The CopyWorkBook: George Washington's Rules of Civility & Decent Behavior in Company and Conversation by Amy M. Edwards and Christina J. Mugglin

The CopyWorkBook: Comedies of William Shakespeare by Amy M. Edwards and Christina J. Mugglin

Other Titles

Hallelujah: Cultivating Advent Traditions with Handel's Messiah by Cindy Rollins

The Birds' Christmas Carol by Kate Douglas Wiggin

The Innkeeper's Daughter by Michelle Lallement

Kipling's Rikki-Tikki-Tavi: A Children's Play by Amy M. Edwards

*These titles are popular with those inspired by Charlotte Mason and her educational philosophy.

Manufactured by Amazon.ca
Bolton, ON